C000302857

FIELD GUIDE TO THE
MUSHROOMS
OF BRITAIN AND EUROPE

First published in 2016 by Reed New Holland Publishers Pty Ltd
London • Sydney • Auckland

The Chandlery, Unit 704, 50 Westminster Bridge Road, London SE1 7QY, UK
1/66 Gibbes Street, Chatswood, NSW 2067, Australia
5/39 Woodside Avenue, Northcote, Auckland 0627, New Zealand

www.newhollandpublishers.com

Copyright © 2016 Reed New Holland Publishers Pty Ltd
Copyright © 2016 in text: Alison Linton
Copyright © 2016 in images: Alison Linton and other contributors as credited

All rights reserved. No part of this publication may be reproduced, stored in a retrieval system
or transmitted, in any form or by any means, electronic, mechanical, photocopying, recording
or otherwise, without the prior written permission of the publishers and copyright holders.

A record of this book is held at the British Library and the National Library of Australia.

ISBN 978 1 92151 773 0

Managing Director: Fiona Schultz
Publisher and Project Editor: Simon Papps
Design and Illustration: Andrew Davies
Production Director: James Mills-Hicks
Printer: Toppan Leefung Printing Limited

10 9 8 7 6 5 4 3 2 1

Keep up with New Holland Publishers on Facebook
www.facebook.com/NewHollandPublishers

Alison Linton

FIELD GUIDE TO THE
MUSHROOMS
OF BRITAIN AND EUROPE

CONTENTS

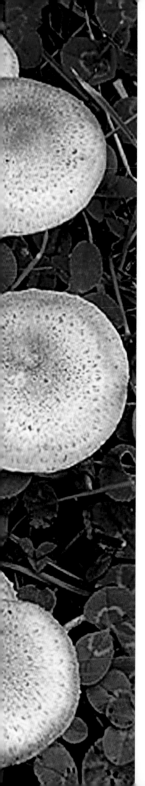

DEDICATIONS

I dedicate this book to:

My son Simon with love

And to my late partner
Christopher Cheshire

ACKNOWLEDGEMENTS

The photographs included in this guide have been extracted from a collection that has taken a decade to amass. Many people have helped me either directly, or indirectly, over these years with my mushroom endeavours and I wish to say a huge and warm thank you to you all. To:

— Simon, my son, for being so incredibly helpful. A decade is a long time and you've been loving and supportive at all times. For being there through all the highs and lows, and for helping to sort out all my computer and technical problems with such grace.

— My dear friend Craig Encer, who spent many hours of his time teaching me how to use Photoshop and to become proficient at managing my website, and for his vision and expertise in helping me to create the Fungiworld website which has led to this field guide.

— Howard Williams, the Recorder for Nottinghamshire Fungi Group (2003–13), who since 2006 has offered me such kind support and encouragement whenever I have requested it. Howard has always made time for me, and his return emails offering me identification help are always detailed and informative.

— Richard Rogers, another member of Nottinghamshire Fungi Group. Richard has been, and still is, a great mentor. He has given me prompt, generous and accurate advice. In particular Richard's help with the difficult task of identifying *Gymnosporangium confusum*, whereby he carried out research and spore print analysis, was very much appreciated, and it was very exciting too.

— Michael and Cornelia Hippisley for their long and loving friendship. They have offered me accommodation and taken me to fabulous locations on so many occasions that I have lost count. All of this support has enabled me to seek out and photograph mushrooms in Scotland.

— Dave Yeomans for buying me a six-inch tripod for those tiny little mushrooms, and for helping to keep me fit and well with regular acupuncture sessions.

— Amy, a member of staff at The Manor Hotel, Exmouth, Devon, who whilst undertaking her shift, so generously lent me her mountain bike so that I could cycle a 14-mile round-trip along the Exmouth coastal path, with the result being that I got to photograph *Bulgaria inquinans*.

— My brother, James Waller, for offering me hospitality and for taking time out of his busy life to take me to some fabulous locations in Surrey.

— Richard English for his cheerful and consistent companionship, and for ensuring my safety when out in remote woods and locations. Also for the fabulous soups and flapjack on those cold winter days.

— Jill Owen for informing me of an unusual fungus in her garden, which turned out to be the rare *Gymnosporangium confusum*, a first record for Nottinghamshire, and for helping me to monitor the situation for six weeks.

— Jackie Ptashko and Hillary Pobal for being such good sports when accompanying me on trips out, and for being so enduring while I take my photographs.

— Anthony Scarfe and Kanchana Minson for their great moral support and encouragement.

— Mark Barrable (Cloudantic IT) for building me a new computer in such a swift and efficient manner, and so ensuring that I was confidently well equipped to write this book.

— Andy Merry, for a truly great friendship and for proof-reading some of the Latin names. Also, for allowing me to use Milford Associates Ltd which hosts www.fungiworld.co.uk so efficiently.

— David Cheshire for his wisdom, and Bettina for willingly helping to proof-read the Latin names.

— My mother, Barbara Waller, for so kindly proof-reading the first draft.

– Richard Mayer for being such a good sounding board and for so promptly and thoroughly proof-reading the entire second draft of the mushroom descriptions.

– Everyone else who I might have met fleetingly and who's names I do not know, who have allowed me to enter their garden or property to take photographs, or helped in some other way.

– To all at Reed New Holland for giving me the opportunity to write this field guide, which is a great honour, and for everything.

INTRODUCTION

This field guide has been written primarily for the beginner to the subject of mushrooms, although it is hoped that it should also be useful for those people with a little more knowledge. There are photographs and descriptions of mushrooms that are common and relatively easy to find, together with a selection of those that are more unusual and rare.

What is a mushroom?

In the most simple of terms mushrooms, and fungi in general, are neither a plant nor an animal and they are often referred to as the 'Third Kingdom,' together with the likes of algae and bacteria. The mushroom structures that the observer sees above the ground are referred to as the fruiting body of certain types of fungi. This fruiting body releases spores and these are spread by various methods, including rain and wind. Some mushrooms 'puff' out their own spores, but whatever the method used, it ensures that the life cycle continues. Mushrooms have what is called a symbiotic relationship with trees, i.e. trees need mushrooms and mushrooms need trees. They exchange nutrients, with each giving the other what it lacks. Mushrooms also play a role in nutrient recycling. They help to return dead matter to the soil so that it can be reused. Without mushrooms there would be massive amounts of dead material lying around.

Mushrooms have many different structures and characteristics and some of the key ones are shown in the 'Illustrations' section.

What is the best time of the year to look for mushrooms?

In general the prime mushroom-hunting season starts in September and ends in March. That is the period of time when the maximum number of mushroom species can be searched for and found. This is a rough guide, however, and suitability varies from year to year, while there are some mushroom species which can be seen all year round. Each year the weather is different. Mushrooms like damp and mild conditions, so the more mild and damp the climate, the better it is for them to grow. A very cold and frosty season will mean there are less mushrooms around to see.

Where do mushrooms grow?

If asked this question most people probably think of an Alice in Wonderland type of habitat. Envisaging a mushroom, or a group of them, growing in grass underneath, or next to, a tree. This is where lots of mushrooms do grow, in forests and woods, but they also thrive, and can be found, in many other types of environment. There are vast and varied places to find mushrooms, such as: in plant pots in greenhouses and in different types of dung, including cow, horse, rabbit and sheep. Other habitats to look at are: allotments; cemeteries; parks; gardens; roadside grass verges; compost heaps; leaf litter; and even old sacking that has been damp for some time. Some mushrooms even grow on the unlikely habitat of old bonfire sites because, for instance, they thrive in the environment of charred wood.

Mushrooms and fungi are sometimes very visible and easy to find. For instance the familiar Fly Agaric, which has a bright red cap, can be spotted from some distance away. Others can be well hidden and patience and persistence, sometimes over a period of many years, is required in order to find them. For example, some might grow inside the hollow of a dead tree trunk, so it pays to poke around and be inquisitive. Some mushrooms are robust, like the large brackets. These take years to grow large and live for a long time. Others are very tiny, also fragile, and can shrivel and vanish within a matter of hours of first appearing.

What colours are mushrooms?

The beginner to mushrooms, and even those people with a little more knowledge, might be surprised to discover the colour range of some mushroom caps. The colours cover a very broad spectrum. There are white, cream, brown and buff-coloured mushrooms, but there are also others with cap colours that are bright red, pink, vivid orange, canary yellow, deep blue, green, purple and black, and some with mixed hues of different colours too. Some stems can also be quite colourful.

What are the different textures of mushrooms?

Mushrooms are very variable in terms of texture. The following are some examples of different combinations of textures that might be encountered, particularly on the cap.

— Smooth and dry, or smooth and damp

— Fibrous/scaly

— Hard/gelatinous

— Warty

— Velvety

— Cracked

What are the different shapes of mushrooms?

Cap shapes

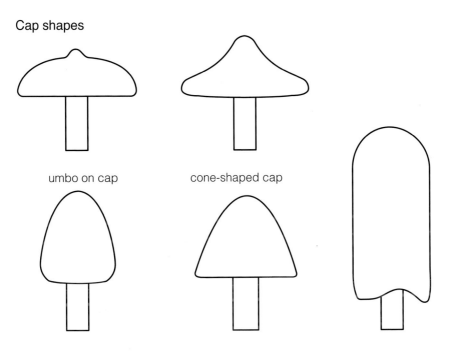

umbo on cap

cone-shaped cap

egg-shaped cap (ovate)

bell-shaped cap

cylinder-shaped cap

Gill structures

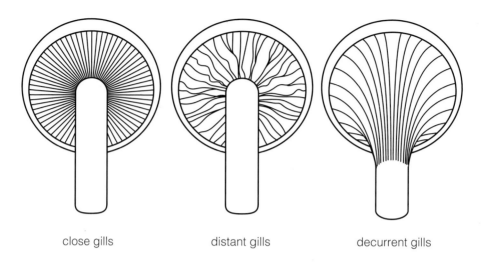

close gills   distant gills   decurrent gills

Pore structures

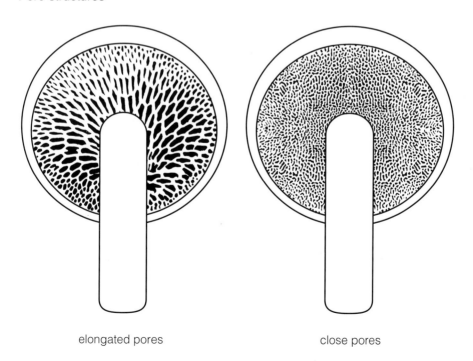

elongated pores   close pores

Types of stem

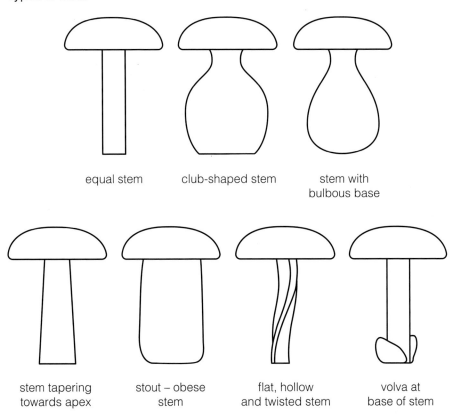

equal stem   club-shaped stem   stem with
bulbous base

stem tapering
towards apex

stout – obese
stem

flat, hollow
and twisted stem

volva at
base of stem

Types of ring

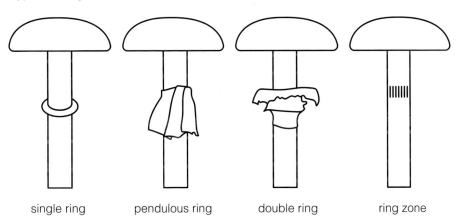

single ring   pendulous ring   double ring   ring zone

What does a mushroom smell like?

Surprisingly, not all mushrooms emit the typical 'mealy' smell expected. Various odours from some mushrooms that may be experienced include almonds, radishes, rotting meat, and aniseed, just to name a few.

Suggested clothing and equipment for mushroom hunting

It is advisable to be prepared for all weathers, and bringing a flask with a hot drink and some snack food is a good idea. A pair of waterproof trousers is a necessity, not only to keep dry, but to protect the lower legs from brambles, thorns and nettles. A pair of gloves is advisable for the same reasons, but to protect the hands and wrists. A small penknife is suggested if you wish to dig out a mushroom for closer inspection. A pocket-size magnifying glass is also helpful for examining the small fibres or scales on the mushroom cap or stem, which can be difficult to see with the naked eye. A small digital compact camera might come in handy if you wish to retain a record of what you've seen, and then do research once back at home. A small notepad and pen are useful for making observations. Finally, a small bottle of antibacterial hand gel is a good idea for cleaning hands after handling mushrooms.

Safety – edibility

Although mushrooms can be seen in gardens and parks, they also grow in isolated and dark environments. Potential risks are posed in dark woods and forests by long trailing brambles, big loose boulders and hidden logs that can become tripping hazards. So care needs to be taken. Also, especially if female, it is sensible to take someone else with you on visits to lonely woods and locations.

I would advise most strongly that none of the mushrooms listed in this guide be eaten, even if listed as edible. Some mushrooms are deadly poisonous. Others can cause gastric upsets or hallucinations. The colours in photographs can vary from the situation in real life, and the reader should attend a professional mushroom foraging outing if wishing to eat mushrooms.

It is hoped that this guide not only helps as a learning tool, but also fosters an appreciation of mushrooms, and that as well as gaining knowledge of the subject, time is taken to pause, and to actually observe the structure. Many mushrooms are beautiful and very photogenic. Some are simply a work of art. Also to be marvelled at, is how these structures actually come to be. Starting off invisible to the naked eye, they evolve into a variety of shapes and forms, whether it be a sturdy bracket attached to a tree trunk, or a minute mushroom with the most delicate cap, managing to push through dry, hard soil, and somehow remaining intact.

And finally, mushrooms are an integral part of our ecosystems but they are under threat from factors such as forest destruction, land-use changes including loss of waste ground and allotments for housing, and climate change. Mushrooms need to be protected and it is hoped that before too long they will be granted conservation status.

ABOUT THIS FIELD GUIDE

The world of mushrooms is vast. Many thousands of types of mushrooms have so far been identified in the UK – in excess of 15,000 varieties – and occasionally new ones are discovered.

At first this world of mushrooms can seem both daunting and complex. There are many terms to learn. For example Latin names, common names and the various structures of mushrooms such as cap shapes, gill types, stem shapes, types of the ring on the stem and so forth.

Therefore, the aim of this book is to introduce the most common species of mushrooms, together with some of the rarer ones, with the help of text explaining their key features, together with over 200 photographs. Each mushroom has a simple and easy to understand written description describing its characteristics, habitat and season. Some mushroom accounts are backed up by two or three photographs – usually those with special characteristics, or those which are unusual in some way.

It is hoped that the guide should equip the reader with enough knowledge to be able to enjoy the thrill of searching for and identifying mushrooms. Once the basics have been learned this should give the reader enough confidence and enthusiasm to explore much more comprehensive guides. Such books will have thousands of mushroom photographs and corresponding descriptions, which are catalogued into Subclasses, Orders and Families. They also include instructions of how to identify mushrooms in a more detailed and scientific way using spore print analysis.

PLEASE NOTE:

The author accepts no legal responsibility for any reactions of any kind to any individual should a mushroom/mushrooms be consumed that is listed in this Field Guide.

ABOUT THE IMAGES

All mushrooms were photographed in Nottinghamshire or Derbyshire, UK, with the exception of the following:

– Angus, UK (*Pholiota squarrosa, Macrolepiota procera, Tricholomopsis rutilans, Hygrocybe conica, Collybia confluens, Panaeolus semiovatus, Lyophyllum connatum, Baeospora myosura, Datronia mollis, Suillus bovinus, Suillus grevillei, Polyporus brumalis, Tremella mesenterica, Calocera viscosa*).

– Cheshire, UK (*Scutellinia scutellata*).

– Devon, UK (*Peziza vesiculosa, Bulgaria inquinans*).

– Killarney, Ireland (*Calvatia excipuliformis, Lycoperdon mammiforme*).

– Norfolk, UK (*Inonotus dryadeus, Geoglossum cookeianum, Tulostoma brumale*).

– Shropshire, UK (*Onnia tomentosa, Trechispora mollusca*).

– Surrey, UK (*Phaeolus schweinitzii*).

COMMON
MUSHROOMS
WITH GILLS

Coprinus comatus

Shaggy Inkcap

DESCRIPTION: This is a tall mushroom. The elongated cap is from 5–15 cm tall; it is at first white, then covered in masses of overlapping darker floccose scales, thus inspiring the alternative name of 'Lawyer's Wig'. The margin can become upturned. The gills are white initially, soon becoming pink and finally black and deliquescing. The stem is up to 30 cm tall, white, strong and smooth and has a white fragile ring that often slips down the stem. HABITAT: In trooping groups on soil, sometimes on grass, roadside verges and garden beds. SEASON: Spring to autumn. STATUS: Widespread. Common. Edible. OTHER NAME: Lawyer's Wig.

ABOVE: *Trooping group*

Pholiota squarrosa

Shaggy Scalycap

DESCRIPTION: Cap diameter 3–10 cm; convex at first, then flattened; it is covered with multiple, coarse upturned scales with the texture being dry. Cap colour begins deep yellow, becoming more ochre with maturity. The gills are pale yellow and crowded, and darkening with maturity. The stem is up to 12 cm tall, tapers slightly towards the base, and is the same colour (concolorous) as the cap; it also has scales below the ring. The ring itself is ragged. Smells of radishes. HABITAT: Found on wood at the trunk base of broadleaf (or rarely coniferous) trees. SEASON: Autumn. STATUS: Common. Not edible.

Coprinus plicatilis

Little Japanese Umbrella Toadstool

DESCRIPTION: Cap 0.5–1 cm across and 1.5 cm tall. The colour is buff initially and then turns pale grey. It has deep grooves with a small cinnamon centre at maturity. The gills are first pale pink and with age turn buff-grey then black. The stem is quite fragile, up to 5 cm tall, narrow and neutral or buff-coloured. HABITAT: Solitary or in small groups, on soil, grass, fields and paths. SEASON: Spring to autumn. STATUS: Very common. Edible.

Coprinus lagopus

Hare's Foot Inkcap

DESCRIPTION: Cap 2–4 cm tall and up to 8 cm in diameter, being grey, shiny initially and when young covered with a grey velvet texture which is the remnants of the veil. At first the cap is cylindrical. It then opens to become rather flat and is covered in light grey fibres. The gills are white, crowded and very quickly turn black and begin deliquescing. The stem is rather tall, up to 10 cm, and bends, being white, covered in a down, and can be swollen at the base. HABITAT: Solitary or scattered on soil amongst leaf litter or bark chippings. SEASON: Summer to autumn. STATUS: Common. Edible.

ABOVE: *Mature example.*
RIGHT: *Young example.*

Coprinus domesticus

Firerug Inkcap

DESCRIPTION: Cap variable in size and can be between 4–10 cm. At first it is elongated and egg-shaped, then more flattened at the margin with maturity. It is pale buff, being initially scurfy-scaly then smooth. The smoothness is most obvious at the centre of the cap and then taking on a grooved appearance towards the margin. As it ages the cap becomes more tawny. The gills are crowded, white then purplish-brown, and finally turning black. The white stem is 4–15 cm tall. It has a swelling near the base which may be darker buff. HABITAT: Grows in groups on wood, logs and twigs of broadleaf trees. SEASON: Spring and summer. STATUS: Common. Not edible.

Coprinus atramentaria

Common Inkcap

DESCRIPTION: Cap 3–6 cm tall. When young it is whitish and egg-shaped. With maturity turns greyish-brown and becomes flattened with an upturned margin. The centre of the cap is more rust in colour with some brown scales. The margin has a tendency to split. The gills are white, then brown, eventually turning black and deliquescing; they are crowded. The stem is white, rather smooth and can be in excess of 10 cm tall, and a ring-like zone may be visible near the base. HABITAT: In small groups in fields, near tree stumps, and near buried wood. Occasionally this mushroom can appear through tarmac. SEASON: Early summer to autumn. STATUS: Common. Edible but best avoided.

Coprinus micaceus

Glistening Inkcap

DESCRIPTION: Cap up to 4 cm tall, firstly oval and then becoming egg-shaped. It is tan-brown, grooved and covered with glistening fine granules, with the margin having a tendency to split. The gills are close, firstly white, and with maturity turning dark brown, finally becoming black and thus eventually deliquescing. The white stem is up to 10 cm tall and is initially felty, but turns smooth as it matures. There is no ring. HABITAT: In small or large groups on stumps of broadleaf trees. SEASON: Late summer to autumn. STATUS: Very common. Edible. NOTE: The photograph of the mature example was taken at dawn, hence the pink hue. The true colour of the glistening granules is shown in the image of the young example.

OPPOSITE: *Young example.*
ABOVE: *Mature example showing glistening granules.*

31

Coprinus disseminatus

Fairies' Bonnets

DESCRIPTION: Cap 0.5–1.5 cm in diameter, being pale buff-grey and convex, then bell-shaped with maturity. It is very grooved and the centre is slightly darker. The gills are crowded, white-greyish and slowly turning black with maturity. These gills do not deliquesce like other *Coprinus* species. The stem can be up to 4 cm tall, is usually white with a fine down, and is curved. HABITAT: In huge groups, up to 50 or more, on wood and old stumps. SEASON: Late spring to late autumn. STATUS: Common. Edible.

Hypholoma fasciculare

Sulphur Tuft

DESCRIPTION: Cap diameter 2–7 cm. The colour is sulphur-yellow with a dark orange shade towards the centre. Firstly it is convex, then more flattened, smooth, often with veil remnants at the margin. The gills are crowded and also sulphur-yellow, but with maturity turn olive-brown and develop a purple tinge. The stem is concolorous with the cap and with time turns darker at the base. It has a fibrous appearance and a faint ring zone. HABITAT: In large groups on the stumps of broadleaf trees. SEASON: All year. STATUS: Very common. Not edible.

Lacrymaria lacrymabunda

Weeping Widow

DESCRIPTION: Cap up to 10 cm in diameter. The colour evolves with age and at first is mustard and then more tan and brown. It is convex when young, later flat and felted with woolly scales. The margin has a ragged appearance. The gills are crowded and dark tan initially, then with maturity become purple-brown and 'weep' in damp weather. The stem is up to 8 cm tall and has a snake-like pattern. It is more or less the same colour as the cap, being more white at the apex. It has a ring zone. HABITAT: On grass in woods and waysides. Tends to be solitary. SEASON: Late spring to late autumn. STATUS: Common. Edible.

ABOVE: *Young example.*
LEFT: *Mature example.*

Pluteus salicinus

Willow Shield

DESCRIPTION: Cap 3–6 cm in diameter, at first convex, then flattened. The cap colour is dark grey, but also tinged bluish or greenish. There is a darker area at the centre. The stem, which is equal in width, can be up to 5 cm tall and usually white, but can also have the colour of the cap at the base. There is no ring. The gills are firstly white, then pale pink, being broad and crowded. HABITAT: Solitary or in small groups on wood of broadleaf trees or rotting stumps, especially willow. SEASON: Spring to autumn. STATUS: Common. Edible.

ABOVE: *Cap.*

LEFT: *Stem and gills.*

37

Macrolepiota rhacodes

Shaggy Parasol

DESCRIPTION: Cap diameter 5–15 cm. Firstly oval, then becoming flattened at maturity. Cap has white background covered with small, dark, brown fibrous scales. The gills are white initially, then bruising with a reddish staining, and are crowded. The stem can be up to 15 cm tall and is white but reddening with age. It tapers upwards towards the cap and has a bulbous base. It has a double superior ring which is usually white but with brown tinges. The ring is also moveable. HABITAT: Solitary or in groups on soil among plant debris and close to conifers. SEASON: Early summer to autumn. STATUS: Common. Edible but can cause stomach upsets in some people.

ABOVE: *Young example.*
LEFT: *Mature example.*

Macrolepiota procera

Field Parasol

DESCRIPTION: Cap 10–25 cm in diameter, being pale buff with scattered darker scales, particularly on the slight broad umbo. The gills are white and crowded. The stem is up to 30 cm tall and greyish-brown and white with patterned snakeskin-type markings. It has a bulbous base. Also it has a very impressive double, superior, moveable ring which is white above and brown below. HABITAT: Either solitary or in small groups in open pastures. SEASON: Late summer to autumn. STATUS: Common. Edible.

ABOVE: *Gills and superior ring.*

Flammulina velutipes

Velvet Shank

DESCRIPTION: Cap is 2–8 cm in diameter, deep yellow and with a slimy appearance. When young it is convex, then flattens, and with maturity turns bright chestnut-orange. The gills are firstly white, then pale yellow, being broad and crowded. The stem is up to 10 cm tall and has a velvet-like texture. It is lighter at the apex, matching the cap colour, then turning brown-red at the base. There is no ring. HABITAT: In clusters on trunks and stumps in deciduous woods. SEASON: Autumn to winter. It should be noted that this mushroom can survive heavy frost. STATUS: Common. Edible.

ABOVE: *Showing velvet texture on the stem.*

LEFT: *Cap.*

Armillaria mellea

Honey Fungus

DESCRIPTION: Cap 5–10 cm in diameter with variable colours, ranging from hues of tan to dark brown. It is covered in minute scales that are darker than the cap. At first it is convex, then flat with maturity. The gills are white at first, slowly turning yellow and then brown as they mature. The stem can grow up to 15 cm tall, tapering towards the base, and has a narrow ring which is yellowish-brown with a cotton-like texture. This mushroom smells mildly acidic. HABITAT: In large clusters on dead wood of deciduous and conifer trees. SEASON: Summer to autumn. STATUS: Very common. Edible when cooked.

RIGHT: *Ring.*

Clitocybe nebularis

Clouded Agaric

DESCRIPTION: Cap 5–20 cm in diameter and cloudy grey in colour, but can also have buff hues. Firstly convex, then with maturity becoming flat with a slightly in-rolled margin. The gills are decurrent, and crowded. They are white at first, and then have a pale yellow appearance with maturity. The stem is up to 10 cm tall and concolorous with the cap. It is stout and has a fibrous appearance and there is no ring. This mushroom can smell fruity. HABITAT: Trooping near conifer trees amongst leaf litter. SEASON: Late summer to autumn. STATUS: Very common. Not edible.

ABOVE: *Gills.*

LEFT: *Group.*

Bolbitius titubans

Yellow Fieldcap

DESCRIPTION: Cap 1–5 cm in diameter, at first pale yellow, then becoming more dull and pale with maturity. It is flat to begin with, then bell-shaped. The texture is sticky and fragile. The crowded gills are pale yellow, then with maturity turn to cinnamon. The stem is up to 10 cm tall and fragile, disintegrating quickly when handled. Close inspection shows a powdery film. HABITAT: Mostly solitary, but sometimes in small groups on manure with straw, and fields, gardens and manured soil. SEASON: Summer to autumn. STATUS: Common. Not edible. OTHER NAME: Yellow Cow-Pat Toadstool.

Lepista flaccida

Tawny Funnel Cap

DESCRIPTION: Cap diameter 5–9 cm. Begins yellowish to tawny in colour but becomes darker with age, and with a sheen when dry. It is flat at first, then becoming funnel-shaped. The gills are very obviously decurrent, broad and pale yellow-cream. The stem is up to 5 cm tall and concolorous with the cap. It is smooth at the apex and white and woolly towards the base. There is no ring. Solitary or in small groups on soil in coniferous woods. HABITAT: In leaf litter in small groups, either near to or under conifer trees. SEASON: Summer to autumn. STATUS: Common. Edible.

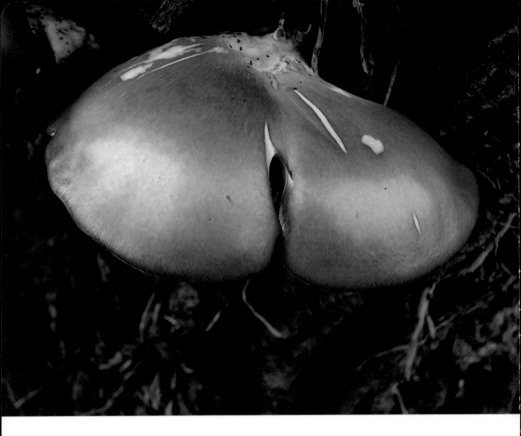

Pleurotus ostreatus

Oyster Mushroom

DESCRIPTION: Cap 6–14 cm in diameter and variable in colour from bluish-grey to brownish-grey to brown. It is lobed or the margin edge can split, and the texture is smooth. The gills are decurrent and are firstly white, then become pale yellow with maturity. The stem is short and stout, being only 3 cm tall; it is white and woolly at the base. HABITAT: Grows on the stumps and logs of broadleaf trees. SEASON: Can be seen throughout the year, but spring and autumn are the best seasons. STATUS: Common. Edible.

ABOVE: *Gills.*

Pleurotus cornucopiae

Branching Oyster

DESCRIPTION: Cap up to 12 cm in diameter. It begins cream and then slowly turns darker with ochraceous tinges. The cap is firstly convex and then flattens out to become funnel-shaped. The margin tends to be wavy, undulating and cracks with maturity. The gills are very decurrent with grooves spreading well down the stem. They are white to pale pink in colour. The stem is up to 8 cm tall and curved, with several caps emerging from one stem; this is also whitish but with age turns the same colour as the cap. This mushroom can smell of ammonia. HABITAT: In large clusters on elm and oak and also other deciduous trees. SEASON: Spring to autumn. STATUS: Common. Edible.

ABOVE: *Gills and branching stem.*

Marasmius androsaceus

Horse Hair Toadstool

DESCRIPTION: Cap 0.5–1 cm in diameter; wrinkled and shaped like a minute parachute. It is pale buff with a pinkish tinge. The centre of the cap has a darker brown hue. The gills are distant and flesh-pink. The stem is up to 6 cm tall, extremely thin and looks like a tough strand of hair. It is very dark brown, shiny and very flexible. HABITAT: In grass in groups amongst pine trees and needles. SEASON: Late spring to autumn. STATUS: Common. Not edible.

ABOVE: *Note distant pink gills.*

Marasmius rotula

Collared Parachute

DESCRIPTION: Cap 0.5–1.5 cm in diameter, white and parachute-like with a ribbed appearance. Centre of cap can turn brown. The gills are broad, white and distant. There is a distinct little collar that can be seen where the stem meets the underside of the cap. The stem can be up to 7 cm tall and is brown, shiny but lighter in colour near the apex; it is very flexible. HABITAT: In large trooping groups on dead twigs in leaf litter. SEASON: Late summer to autumn. STATUS: Common. Not edible.

ABOVE: *Gills and collar.*

Tricholomopsis rutilans

Plums and Custard

DESCRIPTION: Cap up to 12 cm in diameter and has a predominantly yellow background covered with rhubarb-coloured streaks. These streaks are in fact minute fibres or scales. The cap may also have a small umbo. The gills are very deep yellow and broad. The stem is 4–6 cm tall and similar in colour to the cap, but is more yellow than pink. It has a fibrous appearance. HABITAT: In grass near pine forests, or near to conifer stumps. SEASON: Late summer to late autumn. STATUS: Very common. Not edible.

Hygrocybe conica

Conical Waxcap

DESCRIPTION: Cap up to 5 cm in diameter and sharply conical. The margin is often irregular and lobed. It is orange-red and blackens with maturity. The gills are greyish-yellow, quite broad and blacken when bruised. The yellowish stem can be up to 6 cm tall, and this also blackens with maturity. There is no ring. HABITAT: In groups on lawns, grass verges and pastures. SEASON: Late summer to autumn. STATUS: Common. Not edible. OTHER NAME: Witch's Hat.

ABOVE: *Cap with very little bruising.*
LEFT: *Young cap with much bruising.*

Hygrocybe pratensis

Meadow Waxcap

DESCRIPTION: Orange or tawny-buff cap is 3–8 cm in diameter. The cap is waxy but does crack with maturity, and is at first convex, becoming flattened. The gills are deeply decurrent, spaced and buff. The stem is up to 8 cm tall, is much more pale than the cap and tapers towards the base. There is no ring. HABITAT: In groups in pastures, lawns or mown grass. SEASON: Late summer and autumn. STATUS: Common. Edible.

RIGHT: *Deeply decurrent gills.*

Hygrocybe ceracea

Butter Waxcap

DESCRIPTION: Cap 1–4 cm in diameter and yellow, but may be tinged with orange. It looks greasy and becomes flat with maturity. The gills are the same colour as the cap, and are broad and distant. The stem can be up to 4 cm tall and narrows towards the base; it is also the same colour (concolorous) as the cap. HABITAT: In groups in short or mown grass. SEASON: Late summer to autumn. STATUS: Common. Edible.

Collybia confluens

Clustered Toughshank

DESCRIPTION: Cap diameter 2–3 cm; dry, wrinkled and very pale buff to grey, in dry weather it becomes almost white. The gills are close and the same colour as the cap. The stem is up to 6–7 cm tall and also pale buff or grey and with a distinctive flat, and semi-twisted, hollow stem. HABITAT: In small groups amongst leaf litter in pine and mixed woods. SEASON: Summer to late autumn. STATUS: Common. Edible.

Calocybe gambosa

St George's Mushroom

DESCRIPTION: Cap 5–12 cm in diameter, white to cream, with an irregularly wavy margin. Also the margin is slightly in-rolled and the texture is smooth. Gills are crowded and dull white. Stem is up to 5 cm tall and also white or cream. HABITAT: In groups on pastures and sometimes in or near woods. SEASON: Found on or around St George's Day on 23rd April, although can mature a week or so later. STATUS: Common. Edible.

Panaeolus semiovatus

Egghead Mottlegill

DESCRIPTION: Cap diameter 2–6 cm; dull clay to whitish, with irregular creases and drying shiny. The cap of this mushroom remains egg-shaped and never expands. It can have yellow tinges towards the centre. Gills broad and cream, but soon turn black. Sometimes the dark spores can be seen like a powder dusting on the top of the stem. The stem can be quite tall and slender, reaching a height of 10 cm, but can be thicker at the base. It is the same colour as the cap and has a very thin and fragile white ring. HABITAT: In groups on dung. SEASON: Spring to early winter. STATUS: Common. Not edible.

INSET: *Gills.*

Xerula radicata

Rooting Shank

DESCRIPTION: Cap 3–10 cm in diameter and olive to deep brown.
It can be slimy when damp, but when dry it becomes wrinkled. Firstly
bell-shaped and then with maturity it becomes flattened. The gills are
white and broad. The stem is up to 10 cm tall and has a long root, which
is hidden underground and has to be carefully dug out in order to see
it. It tapers and is pale towards the apex, otherwise the same colour as
the cap. There is no ring. HABITAT: Can be solitary or in groups under
or near deciduous trees. SEASON: Early summer to autumn. STATUS:
Common. Edible.

ABOVE RIGHT: *Top of mature cap.*

BELOW RIGHT: *Deep root.*

Amanita rubescens

The Blusher

DESCRIPTION: Cap 5–12 cm in diameter and rosy-brown to pale flesh in colour. This cap can vary in appearance, sometimes having white or pale reddish patches, and occasionally it can have a yellowish hue. When young it is convex and with maturity it flattens out. The gills are crowded, firstly white, and later spotted with red when damaged or bruised. The stem is up to 10 cm tall, with a pronounced bulbous base that is scaly and rough in texture; it is dull white or clay-coloured and has a large membranous ring. Also, the stem becomes more reddish near the base. HABITAT: Can be in groups or solitary in coniferous or deciduous woodland. SEASON: Summer to autumn. STATUS: Common. Not edible.

ABOVE: *Young with pronounced bulbous base.*

Amanita muscaria

Fly Agaric

DESCRIPTION: Cap diameter up to 12 cm. This is a very distinctive mushroom which can easily be seen and identified because of its bright red cap which is speckled with white flecks. With maturity these flecks can be washed off in rain and as the cap fades the colour can turn to a more faded orange. The gills are white and crowded. The stem can be very tall, up to 15 cm; it is also white, predominantly smooth and has a bulbous base. It has a ring at the apex which is also white and large. HABITAT: In groups, usually with birch trees. SEASON: Summer to late autumn. STATUS: Very Common. Poisonous.

ABOVE: *Mature example.*
LEFT: *Young example.*

Paxillus involutus

Brown Rollrim

DESCRIPTION: Cap 5–14 cm in diameter, with an in-rolled margin which remains continuously in-rolled until it dies. The colour of the cap can vary from olivaceous to more rusty-brown; it does darken with maturity and may become dark brown. The cap has a texture that is firm and tough, possibly downy. The example illustrated here has a prominent, acute umbo. The gills are decurrent, crowded and pale rust, eventually turning dark with some spotted rust patches. The stem is up to 12 cm tall, with chestnut staining from the decurrent gills at the apex of the stem. It is equal in width from the apex to the base, and bruises with maturity. There is no ring. HABITAT: Solitary or in small groups on acid soil in broadleaf woodland. SEASON: Summer to autumn. STATUS: Common. Deadly poisonous.

LEFT: *Note the acute umbo on the cap.*

Gymnopilus penetrans

Common Rustgill

DESCRIPTION: Cap 3–8 cm in diameter and golden to tawny-yellow.
Firstly convex, then flattening out and often with a wavy margin; the
texture is smooth. Gills are very slightly decurrent and the same colour
as the cap, but can become tawny-spotted with age. The stem is up to
6 cm tall, more or less the same colour as the cap and can be covered in
a fine white down. There is no ring. HABITAT: Solitary or in groups on
or near conifer wood, sawdust, and stumps. SEASON: Late summer to
autumn. STATUS: Common. Not edible.

ABOVE: *Gills.*
LEFT: *Top of cap.*

Rhodocollybia butyracea

Butter Cap

DESCRIPTION: Cap 4–9 cm in diameter and can be extremely variable in colour, ranging from reddish-brown to pale grey. It is greasy, but when dry a dark grey or brown 'spot' is apparent at the centre of the cap. Crowded gills are pale cream or white. The stem is up to 7 cm tall and is usually the same colour as the cap and tapering towards the apex. The base of the stem might be bent and there is a bulb, which may have white hairs where it enters the soil. HABITAT: Either solitary or in small groups in broadleaf woods, and sometimes in conifer woods. SEASON: Autumn and winter. STATUS: Common. Edible, but eating not advisable.

ABOVE RIGHT: *Gills.*

Inocybe geophylla

White Fibrecap

DESCRIPTION: Cap 1.5–3.5 cm across, conical firstly, then with maturity growing to have a prominent, pointed umbo. Cap white with a yellowish tinge, with the texture being smooth and silky. Gills are crowded, firstly cream and then turning a clay colour. Stem 5 cm tall, also white, with a rather silky texture. There is no ring. HABITAT: In small groups on grass and on the edges of paths in mixed and coniferous woods. SEASON: Early summer to autumn. STATUS: Common. Not edible. Poisonous.

Hygrophoropsis aurantiaca

False Chanterelle

DESCRIPTION: Cap up to 8 cm in diameter and is a lovely yellow to deep orange. On close examination a finely downy texture can be seen. As it matures it becomes funnel-shaped and the margin remains very slightly incurved. The gills are deep orange and decurrent; they are forked, crowded and narrow. Stem is 5 cm tall, the same colour as the cap, smooth and slightly shiny. It can be curved and there is no ring. HABITAT: In groups near to conifer trees. SEASON: Very late summer to autumn. STATUS: Very common. Not edible. Can cause hallucinations.

ABOVE: *Cap showing downy texture.*

LEFT: *Gills.*

Tricholoma scalpturatum

Yellowing Knight

DESCRIPTION: Cap diameter 4–8 cm; very pale grey on a predominately white background, with felty scales. Firstly convex and then flattening out. Gills are white or very pale grey, and a yellow spotting occurs with age. The stem is up to 5 cm tall and white, but can be flushed with the same grey as the cap. HABITAT: In large groups in pine and beech woods. SEASON: Early summer to late autumn. STATUS: Common. Not edible.

ABOVE: *Mature example with yellowing gills.*

Lactarius blennius

Beech Milkcap

DESCRIPTION: Cap up to 10 cm in diameter. It is a mix of colours, being difficult to distinguish as they all merge, but they include greyish, greenish, olive and light grey; slimy when the climate is damp. It is flat at maturity with a depression in the centre. The margin is curved inwards. Sometimes white milk can be seen exuding from the cap where it has been damaged. The gills are a little decurrent, at first white, then turning cream or light buff and being crowded. The stem is up to 6 cm tall, being first pale white, then with maturity turning buff and showing signs of bruising. It is smooth and there is no ring. HABITAT: Solitary or in scattered groups in broadleaf woods, especially beech. SEASON: Summer to autumn. STATUS: Very common. Not edible.

ABOVE: *Cap exuding milk.*

Kuehneromyces mutabilis

Sheathed Woodtuft

DESCRIPTION: Cap up to 6 cm in diameter and appears dark tan in damp conditions, often becoming two-tone from the centre. In dry conditions it appears markedly lighter in colour, and becomes pale ochraceous. Firstly, it is convex and then flattening out with a weak umbo. The texture is somewhat greasy and smooth. The gills are crowded, being pale initially, then with maturity turning cinnamon. The stem is up to 8 cm tall, often curved, being light tan above the ring and darker below; it turns almost black towards the base. The texture is scaly. The ring is dark brown and ragged. HABITAT: In clusters on tree stumps of broadleaf trees. SEASON: Spring to winter but mostly seen in early autumn. STATUS: Common. Although edible this mushroom should be avoided as it closely resembles *Galerina marginata* which is not edible.

UNCOMMON MUSHROOMS WITH GILLS

Hygrocybe nigrescens

Blackening Waxcap

DESCRIPTION: Cap up to 5 cm in diameter and sharply conical. This mushroom has a very vividly coloured cap, being lemon to yellow with streaks of orange and red. With maturity it starts to blacken. The gills are white initially, then pale lemon; they are broad and distant. The stem may be up to 6 cm tall, broad and with streaks of scarlet on a yellow background; this also blackens with age. There is no ring. HABITAT: On short grass in meadows and woodland. SEASON: Late summer to autumn. STATUS: Uncommon. Not edible.

ABOVE: *Mature example.*
ABOVE RIGHT: *Young example.*
BELOW RIGHT: *Gills are broad and distant.*

Hygrocybe calyptriformis

Pink Waxcap

DESCRIPTION: Pinkish-lilac cap 2.5–6 cm in diameter. It can look greasy, but when dry minute fibres can be seen. At first the cap is conical, but it becomes flattened with maturity. The margin is irregular and can split. The gills are pale pink, becoming more white with age and are quite distant. The stem can be up to 12 cm tall and is predominantly white but can flush pink, with a tendency to split lengthways. There is no ring. HABITAT: Usually grows in small groups or is solitary on short grass and pastures. SEASON: Autumn. STATUS: Uncommon. Poisonous.

Pholiota gummosa

Sticky Scalycap

DESCRIPTION: The whitish and yellowish cap is 3–6 cm in diameter.
At first the cap is convex, then with maturity it becomes very flattened.
Spaced-out, large, straw-yellow scales are visible; then as times passes the
cap becomes sticky. The gills are crowded, white, then yellow and finally
reddish-brown. The stem can be up to 7 cm tall, being concolorous
with the cap with a rusty tinge at the base. It has a ring-zone and scales
below that. HABITAT: Either solitary or in small groups on wood, but also
on soil in grass near to conifer trees. SEASON: Late summer to autumn.
STATUS: Uncommon. Not edible.

Lepista saeva

Field Blewit

DESCRIPTION: Cap diameter 6–12 cm; dull brown; begins convex and then becomes flat with a wavy margin. The gills are crowded, at first whitish then turning pinkish-buff with maturity. The stem is up to 6 cm tall and is blue-lilac in colour and with visible fine fibres; it is thick and stout, and may be more swollen nearer the base. There is no ring. This mushroom has a sweet type of aroma. HABITAT: In small groups on soil or chalky pastures. SEASON: Autumn to late winter. STATUS: Uncommon. Edible.

ABOVE: *Stem.*
INSET: *Cap.*

Tubaria conspersa

Felted Twiglet

DESCRIPTION: Cap 0.8–2.5 cm in diameter and either chocolate brown or reddish-brown; it is covered with a greyish velvet-like coating. The stem is quite narrow but equal in width and up to 4 cm tall; it is the same colour as the cap. There is no ring. The gills are close and also reddish-brown with pale edges. HABITAT: Trooping groups in wood chippings. SEASON: Mainly autumn. STATUS: Uncommon. Not edible.

Lyophyllum connatum

White Domecap

DESCRIPTION: Cap diameter 3–7 cm; it has a smooth texture and is pure white, convex at first, then with a wavy margin. Gills are white, broad and crowded; they are also decurrent. The stem is up to 6 cm tall, also white, and often swollen at the base. There is no ring. HABITAT: In small groups on soil in grass in mixed woods. SEASON: Autumn. STATUS: Uncommon. Not edible.

ABOVE: *Gills.*

RIGHT: *Young example.*

Schizophyllum commune

Split Gill

DESCRIPTION: A fan-shaped cap up to 4 cm in diameter; it is whitish and/or greyish and the texture is either 'fuzzy-felty' or finely hairy. The margin is prone to splitting and sometimes there might be a slight purple tinge. The gills are very distinctive as they split lengthways. This fruit body either has very tiny simple stem, which is more or less flat, or none at all. HABITAT: In small groups on dead twigs and wood. SEASON: Throughout the year. STATUS: Uncommon. Not edible.

ABOVE: *Note the distinctive 'split' gills.*

LEFT: *Cap.*

Panaeolus cinctulus

Banded Mottlegill

DESCRIPTION: Cap 2–6 cm in diameter; convex at first and with maturity becomes almost flat. It has a very broad umbo which is darkish red-brown when moist, but dries out to buff to pale tan. The distinctive feature with this mushroom is the darker zone (band) at the margin. The gills are pale tan when young, but rapidly turn darker and eventually black. The stem is up to 9 cm tall, narrow, slender and the same colour as the cap but paler at the apex. There is no ring. HABITAT: In small groups in gardens in compost heaps, manured areas and plant pots in greenhouses. SEASON: Summer to autumn. STATUS: Uncommon. Not edible.

ABOVE: *The banded cap is diagnostic.*

Baeospora myosura

Conifercone Cap

DESCRIPTION: Cap 1–5 cm in diameter and whitish, tan or brown. The gills are also whitish, narrow and very crowded. The stem is up to 6 cm tall and is concolorous with the cap. It is slender, flexible and equal, and the base is covered with hairs. There is no ring. HABITAT: Found rooting on buried pine cones and other coniferous debris. SEASON: Late summer to early winter. STATUS: Uncommon. Not edible.

ABOVE: *Young example.*
ABOVE RIGHT: *Gills.*
BELOW RIGHT: *Note hairy base of stem.*

Agaricus augustus

The Prince

DESCRIPTION: Yellowish-brown cap up to 20 cm in diameter. It is covered in multiple scales which are chestnut-brown; it is firstly convex and then flattens out. The gills when young are whitish to pale pink and with age turn dark brown or even black. The stem is up to 20 cm tall and whitish but has a tendency to bruise pale yellow. There may be some fine scales. It has a large, superior, very broad 'pendulous' ring. This mushroom may smell of almonds. HABITAT: Solitary or in groups on soil below or near broadleaf or coniferous trees. SEASON: Late summer to autumn. STATUS: Uncommon. Edible.

ABOVE: *Note broad ring on stem.*

Leucoagaricus leucothites

White Dapperling

DESCRIPTION: Cap up to 8 cm in diameter, white and very smooth. Firstly convex and then flattens out; as it matures it may become tinged with buff hues. The gills are also white, crowded and turn more buff-coloured with age. The stem can be up to 8 cm tall and is hollow and whitish; it is smooth and has a very fragile and narrow ring near the apex; the base is slightly bulbous. HABITAT: Can be solitary or in small groups in grass verges, gardens and allotments. SEASON: Late summer to autumn. STATUS: Uncommon. Not edible.

ABOVE: *Gills and very narrow ring.*

COMMON
MUSHROOMS
WITH PORES

Trametes versicolor

Turkeytail

DESCRIPTION: A kidney-shaped bracket which can be up to 12 cm across. The fruit body colour is variable with hues of grey, grey-blue, brown or rust; it usually has a white or cream margin. The rough texture is grooved and the colours are in concentric zones. It has pores that are angular in shape. HABITAT: Usually in small to large densely overlapping groups on the dead wood of broadleaf trees. SEASON: All year. STATUS: Extremely common. Not edible.

Trametes gibbosa

Lumpy Bracket

DESCRIPTION: A bracket up to 20 cm in diameter and 8 cm thick. Normally a whitish-grey colour but this bracket is prone to algae growth which gives a bright green appearance. This bracket has minute surface hairs but becomes more smooth with maturity. The texture is cork-like and it can become very hard with age. It has a thick margin. The pores have an elongated appearance and are creamy white. HABITAT: Solitary or in small groups on dead trees, especially beech. SEASON: All year. STATUS: Common. Not edible.

Polyporus squamosus

Dryad's Saddle

DESCRIPTION: A bracket which can grow up to 60 cm in diameter and 5 cm thick; it is flat and fan-shaped with broad dark red to chestnut-brown scales which cover a background of pale ochre. This bracket has pores which are oblong in shape and white. The stem is very short and white. HABITAT: On living and dead trunks of broadleaf trees such as elm and beech. SEASON: From spring to summer. STATUS: Very common. Edible.

ABOVE: *Pores.*

LEFT: *Top of cap.*

Meripilus giganteus

Giant Polypore

DESCRIPTION: Bracket reaching up to 40 cm across and up to 2 cm thick. It is fan-shaped but can also grow in very large overlapping rosettes. It is often finely scaly and the texture corky; the colour is a mixture of light and dark brown. The pores are cream to white, and bruise black with maturity. The stem is usually tiny. HABITAT: Usually at the base of the trunk of broadleaf trees. Sometimes also at the base of roots which are some distance from the tree. SEASON: Summer to winter. STATUS: Common. Not edible.

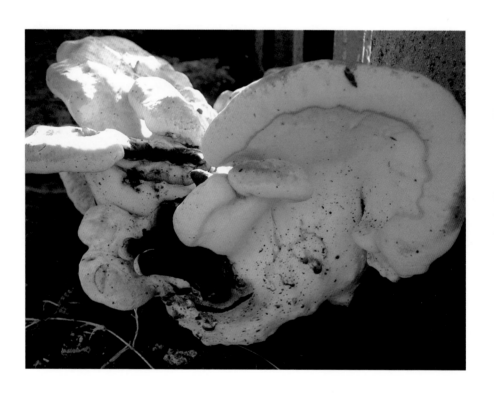

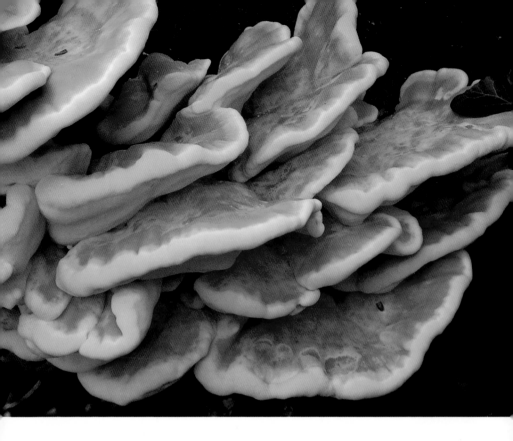

Laetiporus sulphureus

Chicken of the Woods

DESCRIPTION: A very irregularly shaped bracket measuring up to 40 cm in diameter and 1.5 cm thick. It grows in large tiered groups and is very striking, being deep orange with a bright yellow margin and underside. The texture is rubbery and it has a slightly sour odour. The pores are sulphur-yellow. HABITAT: At the base of broadleaf trees, with oak being a favourite, but also found on yew, cherry and apple trees. SEASON: Spring to autumn. STATUS: Common. Edible with caution.

Fomes fomentarius

Hoof Fungus

DESCRIPTION: This bracket can grow up to 25 cm in diameter and is hoof-like in shape, being zoned light and dark grey. It is grooved and hard-textured. The margin is blunt and smooth. Its underside has pores which vary in colour, ranging from light grey to brown and then, with maturity, to cinnamon. HABITAT: Can grow solitarily or in groups and is found especially on birch and also beech. SEASON: Spring to early summer. STATUS: Common. Not edible.

ABOVE: *This example is shown on a fallen log.*

Ganoderma australe

Southern Bracket

DESCRIPTION: A bracket which reaches a diameter of up to 25 cm, and may be just as thick. It is medium brown on the upper surface with concentrical ridges. The texture is hard and inflexible, possibly with some knobbles. The surface of the bracket and the surrounding area can be covered in a thick brown powder which is the dusting of spores. The pores are white or pale yellow to ochre. HABITAT: In plate-like tiers on the lower part of the trunk of deciduous trees. SEASON: All year round. STATUS: Very common. Not edible.

Phellinus igniarius

Willow Bracket

DESCRIPTION: A bracket that is up to 10 cm in diameter and 15–20 cm thick. When young the upper surface is rusty in colour. When it reaches full maturity the upper surface is dark grey and it may even turn black. Firstly it is smooth, and then over time it develops cracks. The margin is pale and clearly defined. Its texture is smooth but tough and hard. The pores are circular and rusty cinnamon in colour. HABITAT: Solitary or in tiers. Mostly on willow but can be seen on other broadleaf trees. SEASON: All year but more common in the autumn. STATUS: Common. Not edible.

ABOVE: *Mature example.*
RIGHT: *Young example.*

Datronia mollis

Common Mazegill

DESCRIPTION: This fruit body grows to 7 cm in diameter and up to 5 cm thick. It grows flat to the bark of trees and consists of a brown upper surface when young, turning black with maturity. It looks like someone has run a comb down the outer surface, thus causing grooves. The pores are angular, elongated and irregularly shaped. These pores are whitish to light greyish. HABITAT: In small groups on dead deciduous wood. SEASON: All year. STATUS: Common. Not edible.

Suillus grevillei

Larch Bolete

DESCRIPTION: Cap diameter 3–10 cm; it is pale yellow but turns rusty coloured with maturity. The pores are also pale yellow, angular in shape and with maturity develop a bruised appearance. The stem is also pale yellow and is up to 7 cm tall; it is equal in width, but sometimes broader at the base and has a whitish ring that is fragile and high up the stem. HABITAT: Solitary or in small groups in grass near larch trees. SEASON: Late summer to autumn. STATUS: Common. Edible.

Suillus bovinus

Bovine Bolete

DESCRIPTION: Cap 3–9 cm in diameter and yellowish with a slimy
appearance; it can also have a pink or ochraceous hue. The margin is
white when viewed from underneath. The stem can be up to 6 cm tall
and is pale yellow; it tapers slightly towards the base and there is no ring.
The pores are large and angular, being an olive-buff then with maturity
turning dark buff. HABITAT: Solitary or in small groups, favouring
Scots Pine and coniferous woods. SEASON: Late summer to autumn.
STATUS: Common. Edible.

OPPOSITE: *Pores.*

UNCOMMON MUSHROOMS WITH PORES

Polyporus brumalis

Winter Polypore

DESCRIPTION: Cap 1–12 cm in diameter with a depression in the middle; the margin is wavy and in-rolled and the colour varies between grey-brown and tobacco-brown, and on close inspection looks minutely bristly. The pores are dull white to cream, and look firstly circular and then elongated with age. The stem is up to 6 cm tall, slender, often curved and yellow to buff in colour. HABITAT: On dead wood of deciduous trees, logs and fallen branches. SEASON: Winter to early spring. STATUS: Uncommon. Not edible.

RIGHT: *The pores become elongated with age.*

Polyporus durus

Bay Polypore

DESCRIPTION: Cap 5–20 cm wide and bay-brown or chestnut with a shiny appearance; it is funnel-shaped and has a thin wavy margin which becomes upturned and thus shows the white pores. As this mushroom matures the cap turns very deep brown, looking almost dark purple. The pores are a dirty white colour, slowly turning pale buff. The stem is almost black, and is short at 2.5 cm tall. HABITAT: In small groups on wood stumps, or on soil. SEASON: Spring to autumn. STATUS: Uncommon. Not edible.

ABOVE: *Mature example with purple hues.*
OPPOSITE: *Young example, chestnut in colour.*

Polyporus varius

Small Black-footed Polypore

DESCRIPTION: This fruit body is up to 10 cm in diameter. It begins kidney-shaped, then becomes flat and depressed; it is striking in having a frilly and lobed margin which might look wrinkled. The colour varies between white and light tan and the texture is corky. The pores are white/cream and circular. These turn brown with maturity. The stem is up to 5 cm tall and is very simple or can be missing. HABITAT: Solitary or in small groups on the dead or dying wood of broadleaf trees. SEASON: Late spring to autumn. STATUS: Uncommon. Not edible.

ABOVE: *The pores begin white and turn brown with age.*

Postia caesia

Conifer Blueing Bracket

DESCRIPTION: A bracket that is up to 6 cm indiameter. When young it is mostly white with hints of blue. As it matures it becomes a darker blue and the upper surface develops fine long hairs. The margin becomes wavy with age. The texture is hard. The pores are white, circular, then angular, and with age slowly turn light blue. HABITAT: In small groups on dead pines and conifers. SEASON: All year but mostly autumn. STATUS: Uncommon. Not edible.

MAIN IMAGE: *Young example.*
INSET: *Mature example with fine long hairs on upper surface.*

134

Phaeolus schweinitzii

Velvet Top

DESCRIPTION: This bracket grows to a diameter of 30 cm and up to 1–2 cm thick. Initially it is dark sulphur-yellow, turning ruddy-brown with hints of red and purple with maturity. When young it has a velvet-like texture. It is zoned and warty and has a bright yellow margin. The pores are olive-yellow then with ageing turn brown. HABITAT: On grass near conifer trees. SEASON: Summer to autumn. STATUS: Uncommon. Not edible.

Inonotus dryadeus

Oak Bracket

DESCRIPTION: A very large bracket that can grow to more than 30 cm in diameter and up to 15 cm thick. When young it is pale grey and with maturity it turns medium rust-brown, while very mature examples can be black. The surface is very uneven and rough in texture. The margin sometimes oozes rusty-red droplets, particularly whilst still growing, although the sighting of these droplets can vary from day to day. The pores are a dirty grey-white and may have patches of rust colour present. HABITAT: Mostly solitary at the base of oak trees. This example was found on a Holm Oak. SEASON: Mostly in autumn and winter, but can be seen throughout the year. STATUS: Uncommon. Not edible.

Grifola frondosa

Hen of the Woods

DESCRIPTION: The fruit body can grow up to 15–40 cm across, being brownish and tongue-shaped with a wavy margin. When dry it takes on the texture and colour of leather. Each branched tongue-shaped cap can be between 4–10 cm across and up to 1 cm thick. The stem is short, cream and repeatedly branches to form the huge fruit body.
HABITAT: Appears at the base of broadleaf trees, mostly oak and beech.
SEASON: Autumn. STATUS: Uncommon. Edible.

JELLY, CUP
AND SIMILAR
MUSHROOMS

Auricularia auricula-judae

Jelly Ear

DESCRIPTION: The fruit body is up to 8 cm in diameter. It is light brown to dark brown with a purple tinge when damp. When the climate is dry it can become brittle and wrinkled. The appearance in normal weather conditions is ear-shaped, with lobes, having a floppy and rubbery texture. The inner surface is smooth and more grey-brown. HABITAT: In small groups and favours elder, but can also be seen on the branches and trunks of other broadleaf trees. SEASON: Throughout the year but more commonly seen in spring and autumn. STATUS: Very common. Edible.

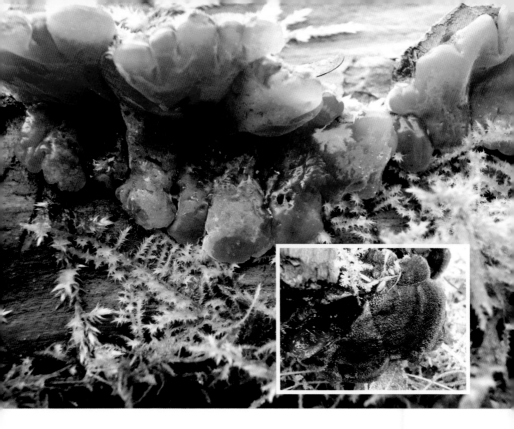

Auricularia mesenterica

Tripe Fungus

DESCRIPTION: Fruit body is up to 6 cm in diameter, grey-brown, has a hairy surface and is wrinkled, wavy and zoned. It grows in tiers in large numbers. The under-surface colour ranges from flesh-coloured to dark purple. It appears gelatinous when damp and hard when dry. HABITAT: On dead and rotting logs and branches of deciduous trees. SEASON: Can be seen throughout the year, but mostly during the autumn and winter. STATUS: Common. Not edible.

INSET: *Showing upper surface.*

Exidia glandulosa

Witches' Butter

DESCRIPTION: The fruit body is 2–6 cm in diameter and virtually black. When young it is disc-shaped, but with maturity it spreads out becoming more floppy and lobed. It has a gelatinous texture, sometimes looking a little shiny, but can become hard and brittle in dry weather. The underside is quite smooth. HABITAT: In small groups on dead logs or branches, favouring oak. SEASON: All year but mostly in the summer and autumn. STATUS: Common. Not edible.

Tremella mesenterica

Yellow Brain

DESCRIPTION: A fruit body that grows up to 12 cm in diameter; it is bright yellow or deep orange, gelatinous and has many lobes. When the climate is damp it is soft, flexible and moist, but it becomes firm and brittle when the weather is cold. HABITAT: Solitary or in small groups on dead and decaying branches of deciduous trees. The example in this photograph was found on gorse. SEASON: All year but particularly in late summer to early autumn. STATUS: Common. Not edible.

Calocera cornea

Small Stagshorn

DESCRIPTION: A yellow fruit body that is quite blunt and not forked at
the tip. The texture is gelatinous with the maximum height being 1–2 cm
tall. As it ages it becomes more orange. HABITAT: In crowded groups
on dead branches and twigs of broadleaf trees. SEASON: Summer to
autumn. STATUS: Common. Not edible.

Calocera viscosa

Jelly Antler

DESCRIPTION: This fruit body can be up to 10 cm tall. It is egg yolk-yellow to orange, with a sticky appearance. Being simply branched, it adheres well to the wood of dead trees. The texture is flexible and tough. HABITAT: On coniferous wood. SEASON: Autumn. STATUS: Very common. Not edible. OTHER NAME: Yellow Stagshorn.

Aleuria aurantia

Orange Peel Fungus

DESCRIPTION: This cup-shaped mushroom is 2–8 cm in diameter; it is bright orange with yellow hues. The texture is slightly scaly but this is only visible with a magnifying glass; it becomes more irregular and folded with age, and turns brittle. When young it resembles a small even-shaped bowl. The internal surface is smooth and the same colour as the outer surface. HABITAT: On bare soil with gravel, by roadsides and sometimes in grass. SEASON: Late summer to autumn. STATUS: Common. Edible.

ABOVE: *Young example.*
LEFT: *Mature group.*

Sarcoscypha austriaca

Scarlet Elfcup

DESCRIPTION: Cup-shaped with a diameter of 1–5 cm. The inner surface is shiny, smooth, and bright scarlet. Upon maturity the margin becomes uneven and might be torn in places. The outer surface is more whitish and with a more rough texture. It has a short stalk. HABITAT: In small groups on dead damp wood or hidden in leaf litter. SEASON: Early winter to spring. STATUS: Uncommon. Seen more frequently in southern England. Edible but poor.

ABOVE: *Young example.*
LEFT: *Mature example.*

Peziza vesiculosa

Blistered Cup

DESCRIPTION: The bowl-shaped fruit body is 3–8 cm in diameter. It is light tan to buff, and on close inspection creased grooves can be seen on the exterior of the cup; also, the exterior is covered in minute granules. The margin is in-rolled, particularly so when young. The interior is smooth and a lighter yellow. When it is dry it can become brittle. This mushroom can withstand frosts. HABITAT: In large groups, specific to horse dung and well-manured soil. The example in the photograph was found in a manured rose-bed in a park. SEASON: All year but more prevalent in late spring and autumn. STATUS: Common. Poisonous.

ABOVE: *Young example.*
LEFT: *Mature example.*

Bulgaria inquinans

Black Bulgar

DESCRIPTION: The fruit body is 1–4 cm in diameter, black, rubbery and shiny resembling liquorice. The margin is tightly in-rolled when young, and it is also more dark brown and less smooth. As it matures it becomes a smooth black disc. The undersurface remains dark brown. HABITAT: In large groups on the dead wood of oak or beech. SEASON: Autumn. STATUS: Common. Not edible. OTHER NAME: Bachelor's Buttons. NOTE: Can be confused with *Exidia glandulosa* (Witches' Butter), which is more lobed and gelatinous.

Geoglossum cookeianum

Black Earth Tongue

DESCRIPTION: A fruit body that can be up to 7 cm tall and up to 2 cm in diameter. It is dull black and looks like an elongated tongue, being smooth and with a blunt and curved tip. The stem tapers from the fruit body and is also black and very short. In dry weather the texture is very brittle. In fact, this mushroom can be very easily missed as it looks like dried black seaweed. HABITAT: In very small groups amongst short grass in sandy soil. Mostly coastal. SEASON: May to November. Uncommon. Not edible. NOTE: This mushroom is similar to *Geoglossum glutinosum* (Glutinous Earth Tongue), but *G. glutinosum* grows in long grass that is not sandy and is shiny and moist in appearance. It is also more rare.

Scutellinia scutellata

Eyelash Cup

DESCRIPTION: The fruit body is 0.2–1 cm in diameter; it is a small scarlet-orange disc, but can look reddish. It has a smooth outer surface and the margin is covered in long pointed hairs, which are dark brown and resemble eyelashes. A hand magnifying glass is useful for seeing these hairs. HABITAT: In groups on rotten wood, often buried in moss. SEASON: Summer to late autumn. STATUS: Common. Not edible.

ABOVE: Close-up of hairs.

Cheilymenia species

Dung fungus

DESCRIPTION: A disc-shaped fruit body which has a small diameter of only 0.5mm. It is bright yellow or orange. It can grow in small or large clusters. There are around 50–60 species of fungus in the genus *Cheilymenia*, and these can only be accurately be identified to exact species by spore print and examination of the eyelash-type hairs around the margin should there be any present. HABITAT: Grows in dung and is more likely to be seen in cow dung. Common in Britain, Ireland and elsewhere in northern Europe. The example in the photograph was found in cow dung that had been lying on an allotment for two months or so. SEASON: Summer to winter. STATUS: Not edible.

PUFFBALL AND EARTHBALL MUSHROOMS

Calvatia excipuliformis

Pestle Puffball

DESCRIPTION: The fruit body is white and the upper part covered in white, pointed, wart-like structures; it is 4–8 cm in diameter and up to 12 cm tall. It is very enlarged at the base, and the base is much broader than the upper fruit body. There is no distinct stem and this mushroom seems to merge into one. HABITAT: Solitary or in small groups in pastures and woodland. SEASON: Late summer to autumn. STATUS: Uncommon. Not edible. OTHER NAME: Long-stemmed Puffball.

Lycoperdon pyriforme

Stump Puffball

DESCRIPTION: A pear-shaped fruit body with a short stem which is covered in tiny warts. It measures up to 5 cm in height and 4 cm in diameter. It is initially white or cream and then with maturity turns brown. Also in maturity, the top of the fruit body develops a hole (pore) by which powder-like spores are released and spread in the wind. HABITAT: In clusters on stumps or pieces of wood. SEASON: Summer to autumn. STATUS: Common. Edible when white. OTHER NAME: Pear-shaped Puffball.

Lycoperdon perlatum

Common Puffball

DESCRIPTION: The fruit body is up to 8 cm tall and 6 cm across; it is white at first when young, and then with maturity turns greyish. It is lightbulb-shaped and covered in coarse warts, particularly on the 'bulb'; these warts do, in fact, rub off. If broken or torn, this mushroom is full of brown-olive powder-like spores. There are no gills. The short stem, measuring about 3 cm, merges into the bulb-shaped head. The apex of the bulb develops a tiny hole to release the spores. HABITAT: In small groups in broadleaf and coniferous forests and woodland. SEASON: Summer to late autumn. STATUS: Very common. Edible when young.

Lycoperdon lividum

Grassland Puffball

DESCRIPTION: The fruit body is up to 3 cm tall and only 2.5 cm in diameter. It is a rather small ochre-brown structure on a pedestal, which is covered with tiny warts and underneath is a faint lined pattern. There is a small pore at the top of the fruit body which allows the escape of spores. A small stem is often hidden in the ground or grass. HABITAT: Grassy dunes, pastures and heaths in sandy soil. SEASON: Summer to autumn. STATUS: Uncommon. Not edible.

Lycoperdon echinatum

Spiny Puffball

DESCRIPTION: The fruit body is up to 5 cm in diameter and 5 cm tall.
It is predominantly mid- to dark brown, with distinctive spines which
can grow up to 6mm long; the spines may eventually fall off and reveal
a matrix-type pattern on the fruit body. It has a small pore at the top
of the fruit body which opens to release spores. The stem merges with
the cap and is very short, being 1.5 cm; this also has some spines on
it and is mid- to dark brown. HABITAT: On soil in broadleaf woods.
SEASON: Summer to autumn. STATUS: Uncommon. Not edible.

ABOVE RIGHT: *Young example.*

Scleroderma verrucosum

Scaly Earthball

DESCRIPTION: The fruit body is up to 5 cm in diameter; it is a dirty brown colour, with a cracked appearance which resembles crazy paving. The texture is leathery. At maturity a hole develops at the top of the fruit body allowing the spores, which are dark brown, to escape. The stem is hardly visible, being only 0.5 cm tall; it has a coarse and ribbed texture. HABITAT: In mixed woods in sandy soil, and also on heaths. SEASON: Summer to late autumn. STATUS: Common. Not edible.

Tulostoma brumale

Winter Stalkball

DESCRIPTION: Cap up to 1 cm across; this is dark cream to pale ochre and is speckled with minute warts. It has a perfectly circular apical pore to allow the escape of spores, but this is so tiny it is easily missed. The stem is up to 4 cm tall and is quite slender and fibrous, being grey or grey-brown and often covered in sand. This tiny mushroom can be easily overlooked as it can be mistaken for gravel. HABITAT: In large groups in moss in coastal sand dunes, specifically in areas with calcareous soil. It is less likely to be seen in northern Britain but occurs widely in mainland Europe, including southern Scandinavia. SEASON: November to April. STATUS: Uncommon. Not edible.

Calvatia gigantean

Giant Puffball

DESCRIPTION: Dimensions highly variable, ranging from 7–80 cm in diameter. The rounded fruit body resembles a ball and is white, smooth and sometimes flaking; it turns brown slowly with maturity and disintegrates over time. It is attached to the ground by mycelial cords, which allow the fruit body to roll about in the wind. HABITAT: Either solitary or in pairs in woodland and parks. SEASON: Summer to autumn. STATUS: Common. Edible when white.

ABOVE: *Mature example.*
RIGHT: *Young example.*

FINGER, CRUST, and SIMILAR MUSHROOMS

Daldinia concentrica

King Alfred's Cakes

DESCRIPTION: Fruit body up to 8 cm in diameter, with a rounded shape like a small ball. It is initially, when immature, a deep reddish-purple, which on maturity becomes greyish-brown or black. The appearance is shiny, hard and smooth. When it is cut in half the internal structure shows concentric rings. HABITAT: In groups and found primarily on beech and ash bark. SEASON: All year. STATUS: Common. Not edible.

ABOVE: *Young pale pink example.*
RIGHT: *Mature example.*

Hypoxylon multiforme

Birch Woodwart

DESCRIPTION: The dark brown to black fruit body has a crust-like texture; it is hard and elongated in shape. It has variable measurements but is normally between 1–2 cm in length and about 1 cm wide. HABITAT: Usually encountered in large masses on the bark of dead branches or birch logs. SEASON: Throughout the year, but mostly in autumn. STATUS: Uncommon. Not edible.

Clavulina rugosa

Wrinkled Coral Fungus

DESCRIPTION: White or cream fruit body is 5–10 cm tall and wrinkled in appearance; it is branched towards the tip, then blunt. The texture is soft, flexible, and may be fragile with bits breaking off. There is no obvious stem. HABITAT: In small groups on soil in leaf litter next to woods. SEASON: Summer to autumn. STATUS: Common. Edible.

Clavulinopsis laeticolor

Handsome Club

DESCRIPTION: Fruit body is 2–8 cm tall, 1 cm in diameter, and bright yellow, but can have orange hues. It is club-like and simple in shape. The tip is blunt and it has a soft texture. HABITAT: Solitary or in small groups on soil or grass in mixed woods. SEASON: Summer to late autumn. STATUS: Uncommon. Not edible.

Clavulinopsis fusiformis

Golden Spindles

DESCRIPTION: This fruit body is bright yellow, slender and up to 10 cm tall. There is no stem as such and it can look grooved. The tips are very pointed and are yellow when young but turn brown with maturity. It has a firm texture. HABITAT: In small groups on soil in pastures and grassland or mixed woods. SEASON: Late summer to autumn. STATUS: Common. Not edible.

Clavaria fragilis

White Spindles

DESCRIPTION: Fruit body 6–12 cm tall. It is a white structure best described as a simple club, being mostly straight and upright. It can, though, become wavy. As it matures the very tips become discoloured and turn yellow. It may also have grooves appearing from the tip to the base. The texture is mostly soft but turns brittle when dry. HABITAT: In small groups in fields, grassy clearings, leaf litter and on the edge of woodland. SEASON: Mid-summer to early winter. STATUS: Uncommon. Not edible.

Xylaria hypoxylon

Candle Snuff Fungus

DESCRIPTION: A fruit body that is up to 6 cm tall and black with a white tip. It is branched and looks like a burnt matchstick. With maturity the white tip disappears, leaving a dry, brittle stalk. HABITAT: In groups on the dead wood of broadleaf trees. SEASON: All year but mostly during the summer to autumn. STATUS: Common. Not edible.

Xylaria polymorpha

Dead Man's Fingers

DESCRIPTION: Fruit body black when mature and protrudes from stumps of trees. Each of the finger-shaped structures is blunt, from 3–8 cm tall and 3 cm wide, and is varying shades of brown when young, turning black when mature. The texture is hard, tough and rough, with fine wrinkles sometimes visible. The stem is more like a narrow stalk. HABITAT: Stumps on or near beech. SEASON: All year. STATUS: Common. Not edible. NOTE: This photograph shows a young example prior to turning black.

Xylaria longipes

Dead Moll's Fingers

DESCRIPTION: Fruit body very similar to *Xylaria polymorpha* (Dead Man's Fingers), but the fingers are more slender and are also prone to bending slightly. It is up to 8 cm tall, overall more slender, club-shaped and tapering into a cylindrical stalk. It is black and finely wrinkled. The small stem is more brown in colour. HABITAT: In small groups on stumps and fallen branches, mostly of sycamore. SEASON: All year, but can be seen more frequently in the summer and autumn. STATUS: Common. Not edible.

Macrotyphula fistulosa

Pipe Club

DESCRIPTION: This very pale yellow to cream fruit body can reach a very tall 30 cm in height; it has a simple structure and is very slender, being only 0.2–0.8mm in diameter. Some of the tips are acute, then blunt, and a few can become flat at the apex, taking on the appearance of a crochet hook. HABITAT: In groups well-hidden on the ground in leaf litter on the twigs of deciduous and conifer trees. SEASON: Autumn. STATUS: Uncommon. Edible but poor.

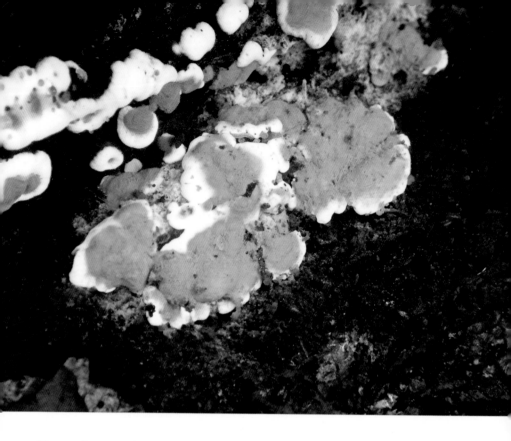

Kretzschmaria deusta

Brittle Cinder

DESCRIPTION: Fruit body is battleship-grey to whitish and irregularly shaped. It can reach up to 10 cm in diameter and is like a small, uneven, firm cushion. With maturity it eventually turns black, becomes very brittle, and can be crushed when rubbed together. HABITAT: On old dead stumps of deciduous trees. It can also be well hidden in the hollows of old stumps. SEASON: Summer and autumn. STATUS: Common. Not edible.

Biscogniauxia nummularia

Beech Tarcrust

DESCRIPTION: Fruit body black, shiny and hard with a crusty structure. The area it covers is variable. HABITAT: Dead wood of beech trees. Occurs in clusters and merging into one, with a cracked appearance. SEASON: Throughout the year, but mostly in autumn. STATUS: Common. Not edible.

Nectria cinnabarina

Coral Spot

DESCRIPTION: Fruit body approximately 0.5 cm in diameter; it consists firstly of cinnabar-red small masses which over time turn coral-pink. Closer inspection with a hand lens shows that these masses look like small cushions. HABITAT: In large clusters on dead wood. SEASON: Throughout the year. STATUS: Very Common. Not edible.

RIGHT: *Cinnabar-red masses.*
ABOVE: *Mature coral-pink masses.*

RARE AND
UNUSUAL
MUSHROOMS

Lycoperdon mammiforme

Flaky Puffball

DESCRIPTION: A rather small fruit body that is 3–5 cm in diameter and up to 5 cm tall. It is white when young and slowly turns light brown as it matures. The fruit body is a rounded structure with woolly patches that take on the appearance of a golf ball with raised bumps. At the top of the fruiting body a pore develops so that spores can be released. The stem is more like a pedestal and is short. HABITAT: Favours chalky soil under broadleaf trees. SEASON: Autumn. STATUS: Rare. Not edible.

ABOVE: *Close-up of structure.*

Onnia tomentosa

Velvet Rosette

DESCRIPTION: Dirty yellow-orange cap up to 10 cm in diameter; it is flat when young, later having a slightly depressed centre and becoming raised at the margin edge. When touched the cap has the texture of a peach; it can have two layers and is covered in felt that is greyish-brown when young, then becomes yellowish. The stem is up to 7 cm, dark brown to black, minutely felty (tomentose) and is not always centrally attached to the cap. HABITAT: Coniferous forests. Can be found in large groups or solitary. Mostly found at higher altitudes; rarer at lower altitudes. SEASON: Late summer to autumn. STATUS: Uncommon/rare. Not edible.

ABOVE: *Close-up of texture.*

Stereum subtomentosum

Yellowing Curtain Crust

DESCRIPTION: The fruiting body is colourful, being a mixture of grey
and bright orange-rust in zones, although has a tendency to turn green
with algal growth. Each fruit body can be up to 7 cm in diameter but it is
rather thin. Flexible when damp but becomes hard and brittle when dry.
The underside is smooth. HABITAT: On dead wood of broadleaf trees.
SEASON: All year. STATUS: Rare. Not edible. This mushroom is larger
than the other species in its group.

Trechispora mollusca

(no common name)

DESCRIPTION: The dimensions of this fruit body are variable as it spreads irregularly, but the thickness is less than 1 cm. It is not securely attached and is finely porous with fringed edges. The texture is soft. At first it is pure, bright white, and it becomes more brown with age.
HABITAT: The undersides of both coniferous and broadleaf logs.
SEASON: Mostly in summer and autumn. STATUS: Common. Not edible.

Volvariella bombycina

Silky Rosegill

DESCRIPTION: Cap 8–20 cm in diameter, white and covered in yellow-tinged fibres, which are long, silky and overhang the margin edge; the fibres resemble short sheepswool and feel soft to the touch. The gills are white, broad and close; with maturity they turn flesh-pink and then dull brown. The stem can be up to 15 cm tall and is often curved; it is white with minute white scales. There is no ring and the base is surrounded by a volval bag. HABITAT: On dead branches and hollow trunks of broadleaf trees. SEASON: Late summer to autumn. STATUS: Rare. Edible.

ABOVE RIGHT: *Volval bag.*
BELOW RIGHT: *Close-up of fibres.*

Pholiota flammans

Flaming Scalycap

DESCRIPTION: Bright yellow cap 4–8 cm in diameter and with upturned lemon-yellow scales which can overhang the margin edge. The gills are crowded and also yellow and become darker with maturity. The stem is concolorous with the cap and just as scaly, and can be up to 10 cm tall. It has a ring which is also yellow and close to the apex, which is ragged and difficult to see amongst all the scales. HABITAT: Solitary or in small groups on stumps of conifer trees. SEASON: Late summer to autumn. STATUS: Rare. NOTE: The example in the photograph was hidden under leaf litter.

ABOVE: *Overhanging scales on cap.*
OPPOSITE: *Scaly stem.*

Phaeomarasmius erinaceus

Hedgehog Scalycap

DESCRIPTION: Cap diameter 1–1.5 cm. Ochre-tan with a reddish hue, but the margin is more pale. It is very scaly, the scales pointed, and when young it has a fringed margin. The stem is tiny, being only up to 2 cm tall, and is mostly curved, scaly, and slightly darker than the cap. There is no ring. The gills are rather distant and initially the same colour as the cap, but becoming rust-coloured with age. HABITAT: Solitary or in small groups on willow. SEASON: Throughout the year, but mostly seen in late summer and autumn. STATUS: Uncommon to rare. Not edible.

ABOVE: *Gills.*

Amanita strobiliformis

Warted Amanita

DESCRIPTION: Cap 6–20 cm in diameter, pure white and covered with many flat, light grey scales which eventually overhang the margin. The gills are also white and crowded. The stem can grow to 10 cm tall, is also white and is shaggy at maturity, otherwise having a rough texture with remains of a volval bag at the base. It has a large ring that is thin and superior. HABITAT: Usually solitary on soil near broadleaf trees. SEASON: Summer to autumn. STATUS: Rare. Never to be eaten as easily confused with other mushrooms which are deadly.

ABOVE: *Young example.*
LEFT: *Gills.*

Mycelium

This image shows exposed mycelium, which is the vegetative body of most fungi and is normally hidden from view. It consists of branching threads that are found in and on soil or other habitat. This photograph shows mycelium on a dead log where a chunk had fallen off, thus exposing the normally unseen network.

RIGHT: *Close-up.*

Gymnosporangium confusum

Juniper Rust

DESCRIPTION: Diameter 2–4 cm. Medium brown with orange speckles. Forms a ball-like gall (an outgrowth), and this then produces a set of orange tentacle-like spore tubes called telial horns. These horns expand and have a jelly-like consistency which when wet may also fall to the ground as individual clumps. The spores of this fungus can travel a few miles in the wind and can then infect other trees, including apple, pear or hawthorn. This fungus does not cause damage to juniper trees, but can do so to apple and pear trees, and therefore seriously affects the production of fruit. HABITAT: Found on Chinese Juniper trees. SEASON: Early summer. STATUS: Rare. Not edible.

ABOVE: *Fungus on tree.*

LEFT: *Example of the jelly-like consistency which has fallen to the ground.*

207

Arrhenia retiruga

Small Moss Oysterling

DESCRIPTION: Cap 0.5–1.5 cm diameter. A difficult fungus to find due to its small size and habitat. It is disc-shaped, or like a fan. The colour is whitish to pale grey and the margin is lobed. On careful inspection it looks wrinkled, with the wrinkles spreading from the centre. This fungus is unusual in that it has no stem or gills, and looks like it is just resting on either grass stems or moss. HABITAT: In clusters, usually on moss. Occasionally on dead grass or twigs. SEASON: Winter to spring. STATUS: Uncommon. Not edible.

Rhodotus palmatus

Wrinkled Peach

DESCRIPTION: Cap diameter 5–7 cm, pale pink at first, then with age it turns a more peach/apricot colour; it is firstly convex then flattened, and has a smooth texture, but is also gelatinous with a slight in-rolled margin. As it matures it becomes very wrinkled. The gills are often paler than the cap and are narrow, close and interconnected/veiny. The stem is up to 5 cm tall, often curved and is also pinkish and may have some white fibres. There is no ring. When young, the stem can exude blood-red droplets. HABITAT: Solitary or in small groups on elm logs. SEASON: Early autumn to winter. STATUS: Rather rare due to lack of elm trees after Dutch elm disease. Not edible.

Ganoderma lucidum

Lacquered Bracket

DESCRIPTION: A bracket that can be up to 30 cm in diameter and 3 cm thick. It is ruddy-brown, shiny, and looks as though it has been varnished, with a paler margin; it is grooved and zoned and is fan- or kidney-shaped. The pores are circular, at first white, and then with maturity turn tobacco-brown. The stem is very short, being approximately 3–5 cm, and is also shiny and dark brown. HABITAT: Grows close to the ground on roots of mostly oaks, but also other broadleaf trees. SEASON: All year but mostly summer to autumn. STATUS: Rare. Not edible.

ABOVE: *Pores.*

Geastrum striatum

Striate Earthstar

DESCRIPTION: A fruit body that consists of a bulb situated on top of a star-shaped base, with finger-like projections knows as 'rays'. When young the unopened bulb might be up to 4 cm in diameter and when opened at maturity the whole fruit body might be up to 6 cm in diameter. The bulb is dull grey with a beak-like apex. There is a small 'collar' type of structure and the bulb rests on a short thin stem, approximately 5mm long, which connects the bulb to the star-like rays that rest on top of the ground. The rays are coarse, scaly and brownish-grey, and there may be between six and nine. As the fruit body matures the bulb becomes more fragile, thus allowing spores to be released. HABITAT: Mostly solitary but sometimes in groups on soil amongst leaf litter near broadleaf or coniferous trees, and also hedgerows near rotting stumps. The example in the photograph was found on an allotment. SEASON: Late summer to autumn. STATUS: Rare. Not edible.

Helvella lacunose

Elfin Saddle

DESCRIPTION: Cap 2–5 cm in diameter and dark grey to black with up to two distorted and irregular lobes that can be crumpled. The cap has a wavy margin which is fused with the stem. There are no gills or pores, but a smooth underside. The pale grey hollow stem is 3–10 cm tall, stout, tapers upwards and has deeply grooved furrows. Holes may also appear in the stem at maturity. HABITAT: In small groups or solitary on soil in broadleaf, coniferous or mixed woods, often on burnt ground. SEASON: Autumn. STATUS: Uncommon. Edible but poor quality.

Phallus impudicus

Common Stinkhorn

DESCRIPTION: This fruit body begins life as a white, small, round egg, being rubbery in texture and up to 6 cm in diameter. It is usually half-buried in the soil and is attached to the ground by a strong rubbery cord which is mycelial. From this egg emerges a mushroom which can reach up to 20 cm in height. The 'head' is matrix-like in structure, but is covered in an olive-green to brown slimy mass which smells very unpleasant (like raw sewage), and which is evident many metres away from the mushroom. This slimy mass attracts flies which spread the spores. The stem protrudes from the ruptured egg and is white and up to 8 cm tall, with a net-like appearance. HABITAT: Gardens and deciduous woods. Usually solitary. SEASON: Summer to late autumn. STATUS: Very common. Edible at the egg stage.

ABOVE: *Fungus with remains of egg on cap*

OPPOSITE: *Egg from which fungus emerges.*

RIGHT: *Matrix remaining when mass has disappeared.*

Ramaria stricta

Upright Coral

DESCRIPTION: A fruit body that is up to 10 cm tall and 8 cm wide. It has many upright branches which are ochraceous but can also look flesh-coloured; these all start at a small but strong pale stem that is less than 2 cm in diameter. With age the fruit body becomes darker and is prone to bruising. Also, it has a sweet smell of pepper and aniseed. HABITAT: On the ground around conifers. SEASON: Late summer to winter. STATUS: Uncommon. Not edible.

GLOSSARY

Apex	towards the top of the stem
Attached	referring to a ring attached to a stem
Bracket	mushrooms that are plate-like and grow in tiers
Bulbous	stem with a swollen bulb-shaped base
Cap	the flat or umbrella-shaped cup on top of the mushroom stem
Clavate	club-like stem
Close	a narrow gap between each gill
Conical	cone-shaped cap
Concolorous	the cap and stem being the same colour
Convex	cap turning upwards/outwards
Decurrent	gills running down to the stem
Deliquescence	after maturity becoming liquid
Distant	a wide gap between each gill
Double	two distinct rings on the stem
Eccentric	a stem not central to the cap
Equal	a stem that is the same thickness from apex to base
Floccose	covered in cotton-like strands
Fruit body	the visual part of the mushroom that arises

Gill	the structure found on the underside of the caps of mushrooms having gills
Inrolled	cap that is rolled inwards
Irregular	a cap that is irregularly shaped
Margin	outer edge of the cap
Milk	a white juice either seen as droplets on a cap or when the cap is cut with a knife or broken
Mycelium	the hidden strand-like structure of a mushroom that is mostly underground
Movable	refers to a ring on a stem that can be moved up and down
Partial	as in veil. Referred to as a partial veil, which is a protective layer that joins the edge of the cap to the stem
Pendulous	(as in ring on stem) hanging loosely and freely
Pore	a small hole on the underside of mushrooms that can be round or elongated in shape and where spores can be excreted
Ring	1. the remains of the partial veil found on the stem on a mushroom
	2. groups of mushrooms that grow in circles on lawns or in soil
Ring zone	a very faint mark where the ring has been
Rooting	where a stem grows deeply in the ground in a root-like manner

Rust	some fungi that have a complex lifecycle and can infect plants
Split	as in a cap that has a split margin
Spore	the reproductive, microscopic body of the mushroom. A single cell and variable in shape
Stipe	another term used for the stem of a mushroom
Troop	a group of mushrooms appearing close together
Umbo	a raised bump in the centre and on top of the mushroom cap
Volva	a bag-like structure covering the base of the stem
Wavy	the outer edge of the cap (margin) having an irregular or wavy appearance

INDEX

Other Natural History titles by Reed New Holland include:

1,000 Butterflies
Adrian Hoskins
ISBN 978 1 92151 756 3

Bugs in Close-Up
Colin Hutton
ISBN 978 1 92151 738 9

Meerkats
Grant Mc Ilrath
ISBN 978 1 92151 765 5

Owls of the World
James Duncan
ISBN 978 1 92151 764 8

Raptors In Focus
Dick Forsman
ISBN 978 1 92151 768 6

Seabirds of the World
David Tipling
ISBN 978 1 92151 767 9

Top Wildlife Sites of the World
Will and Natalie Burrard-Lucas
ISBN 978 1 92151 759 4

Volcano Discoveries
Tom Pfeiffer and Ingrid Smet
ISBN 978 1 92151 735 8

Wildlife On Your Doorstep
Mark Ward
ISBN 978 1 92151 774 7

World's Deadliest Creatures
Joe and Mary Ann McDonald
ISBN 978 1 92151 776 1

For details of these and hundreds of other Natural History titles see www.newhollandpublishers.com